DECORATIVE FLORAL DESIGNS

for Needleworkers and Craftspeople

by JEHAN RAYMOND

Dover Publications, Inc., New York

Publisher's Note

Jehan Raymond's *Le Cuir: Compositions Décoratives* ("Leather: Decorative Projects"), published in Paris about 1906, originally consisted of 48 color halftone plates detailing projects for leatherwork decoration: cigarette boxes, letter openers, picture frames, napkin rings, hand mirrors, etc. To facilitate transfer for executing the projects, each plate had a tissue overlay with line renditions of the motifs. These line renditions are the designs that are reproduced in this book. Most are florals reflecting the influence of Art Nouveau, whereas some depict people, landscapes and animal and insect life. Monograms, originally scattered throughout, are here grouped together. The quality of these designs is such that they are easily adaptable for any number of crafts—needlepoint, leatherwork, pyrography—or for line art in graphic projects.

Published in Canada by General Publishing Company, Ltd., 30 Lesmill Road, Don Mills, Toronto, Ontario.
Published in the United Kingdom by Constable and Company, Ltd.

This Dover edition, first published in 1986, is a selection of line illustrations from the portfolio *Le Cuir: Compositions Décoratives,* as published by Librairie Renouard, Paris, ca. 1906. A Publisher's Note has been written specially for the present edition.

DOVER *Pictorial Archive* SERIES

Manufactured in the United States of America
Dover Publications, Inc., 31 East 2nd Street, Mineola, N.Y. 11501

Library of Congress Cataloging-in-Publication Data

Raymond, Jehan.
Decorative floral designs for needleworkers and craftspeople.

(Dover pictorial archive series)
Illustrations reprinted from: Le Cuir. Paris : Libr. Renouard, ca. 1906. With publisher's note.
1. Decoration and ornament—Plant forms. 2. Leather work. 3. Needlework. I. Title. II. Series.
NK1560.R35   1986   745.4   86-6242
ISBN 0-486-25134-9

4

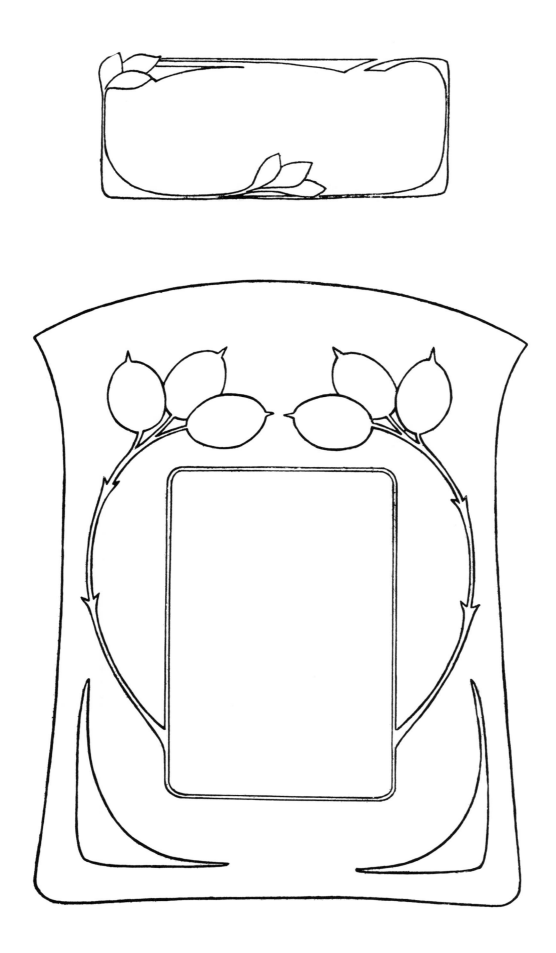

13

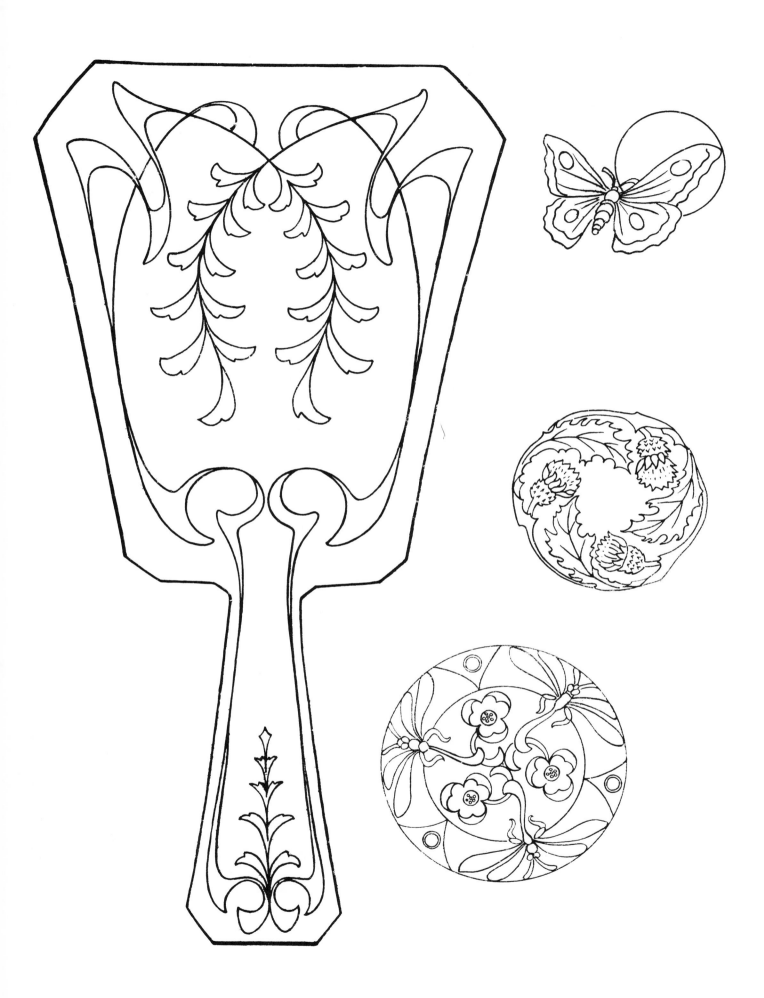

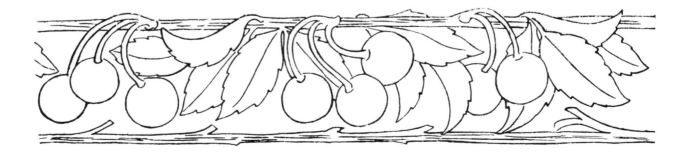

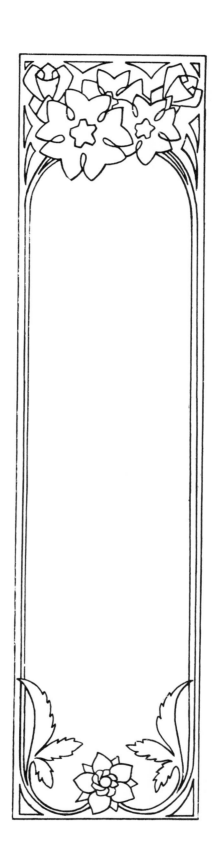

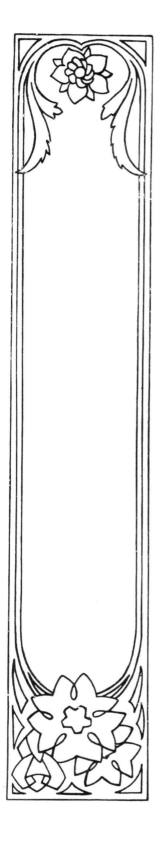

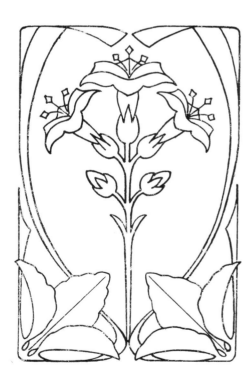

29

31

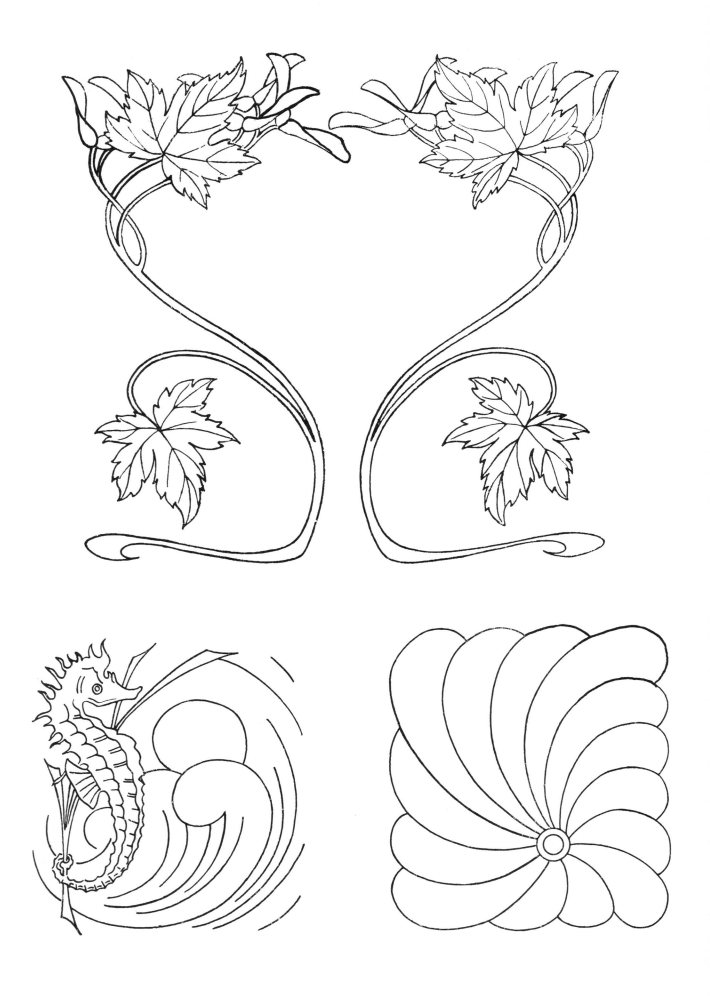

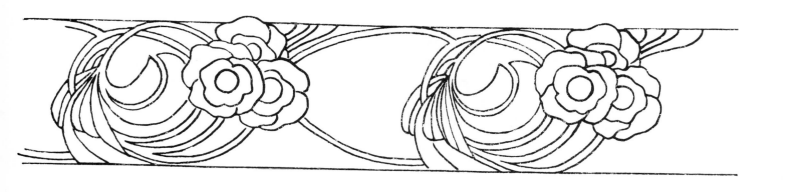

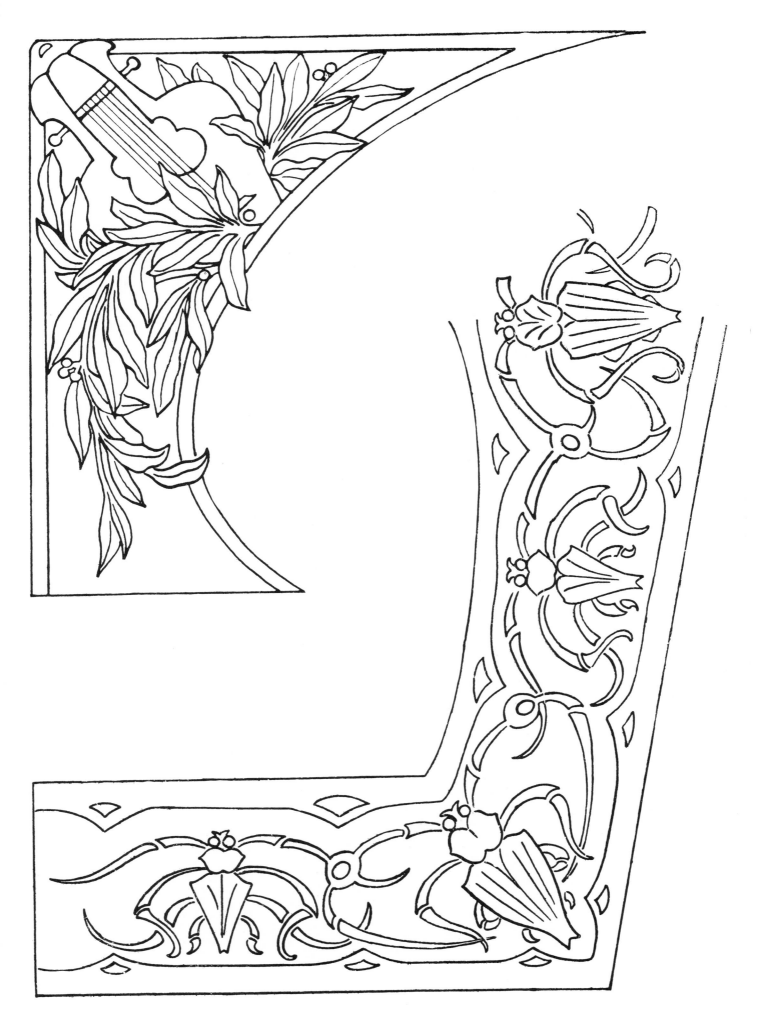

49

50

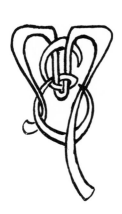